ISBN: 978-1-7397577-8-6

NICK REEVES & INGRID WILSON

Archery In The UK

Nick Reeves rents an attic in the upper east corner of North Tyneside. If he squints, the North Sea rattles the weirdoes. He hums a vague melody and pockets paper scraps and treasure found in the street. He counts every magpie that he sees; last tally, 10. Which is not to be missed. His most recent publication credits include a chapter in *Nothing Is More Real Than Nothing* (Valley Press, 2022), Gleam's Journal of the Cadralor (Issues IV and V), and Free Verse Revolution (Issue VIII).

Ingrid Wilson walks as she writes, and writes as she walks: sometimes rambling, often too fast, but always with purpose. She inhabits the Northlands and roams the borders looking for ley lines and keywords. She also publishes books. Her most recent publication credits include Free Verse Revolution (Issue VII), Gleam's Journal of the Cadralor (Issue IV), and her debut poetry collection, *40 Poems At 40* (EIF, 2022).

Praise for Archery In The UK

"If you are you looking for a poetry collection that will put a huge smile on your face, this is the book for you. Ingrid Wilson and Nick Reeves have created a book of contemporary lyrical poetry, the likes of which I haven't seen."

— Barbara Harris Leonhard, Editor, MasticadoresUSA.

"Reading *Archery in the UK* left me with a strong feeling of sau-dade that stayed with me long after I'd finished the book—which is the best recommendation I can give to encourage other readers to experience this remarkable volume of collaborative poetry."

— Elizabeth Gauffreau, author of *Grief Songs* (Paul Stream Press, 2021)

"Archery in the UK is a true delight. It is a joy to read. We journey with these lovers, feel their sorrow and happiness—and witness the growth of their love."

— Merril D. Smith, author of *River Ghosts* (Nightingale and Sparrow Press, 2022).

"This collection is a beautiful love story, blooming with rhythm and metaphor...These poems are original, gorgeously entwined yet universal."

— Kristiana Reed, Editor, Free Verse Revolution.

ARCHERY IN THE UK

NEW LYRICAL BALLADS
AND OTHER POEMS
BY

NICK REEVES &
INGRID WILSON

Contents

1. Tend toward magic realism; the natural, the supernatural. 2. Eschew cliché, bandwagon & first draft. 3. Embroider! Embrace! Embody! 4. Blend language with landscape and vice versa. 5. Hike hill and lake, comb beach and page. Take to tarmac, to barricade, to battlement, to barrow. Encircle cathedrals and castles, clockwise and widdershins. 6. Experiment – with form, narrative and structure; be it sonnet, ballad, pantoum, postcard. 7. Collage, tesselate. 8. Cajole, conjure, create. Excellence is your goal. 9. Romanticists, nurture the dream state of mill and attic. 10. Declare this day a poets' weekend! (from *Manifesto For The New Lyricists*, 2023)

"Come forth, and bring with you a heart
That watches and receives."

— William Wordsworth, 'The Tables Turned' (from *Lyrical Ballads*, 1798)

Prologue

We stood behind the barricade,
the battlements, the barrows,
and, with our bowmen's hearts we laid
a wooden rain of slant arrows.

And the arrow arched the blue and fell
their voices dimmed and faded.
The wave rose silent in the bay.
The needle and the vinyl braided.

And supine upon the shore, the boy became
quite calm — resigned, unseaming.
Unheard, the unholy crowd proclaim
that all before this time was dreaming.

The Archer's Postcard

i.

The storm debris of yesterday draws a leitmotif
of poems from the ordinary eddies on the stream.
Beneath Newcastle Christmas lights, a confederacy
of dreamers breeze the streets of King and Queen.

There is also synchronicity — this being the Eve
of Saint Nicholas ('… archers and repentant thieves') –
I see one glove in need of another, and another on the quay;
two mirrors between stories in the Baltic Gallery.

ii.

There is a quiet to the mill; not silence
quite; not quite, but, still
enough to keep real life in abeyance.

iii.

The art is mostly hopeless and best avoided before pizza:
although a water coloured, pen and ink —
study of a kingfisher —
on the 3rd floor, by the rivered window,
is delightful.

The tea in the cafe is pay-as-you-please.

(De)parting

I walked east the Grainger Street rain
your train west had long departed
Byker, Meadow Well, Percy Main
but the clouds remained unparted.

Winter Love

The glitter of frost lit up the sleeping land
while in the terraced houses, children slept.
The choir of angels tuned up like a band
piping their song of joy, a promise crept

into my mind, as I lay all alone
but did not feel it, for my heart that night
had been transformed from a vessel of stone
into an organ pumping pure delight

all through my body, all throughout my veins
stirring to life, the wild elixir ran
obliterating memories of past pains
as a new chapter in my life began:

And so, I wrote down these brief lines to you
daring to dream that you might feel it too.

Night Falls

Night falls upon the frozen mountain-land
hardy tufts of grass lit in gold green
an empty hand in glove, an empty hand
holds onto nothing bigger than a dream.

Hardy tufts of grass lit in gold green
ignite the hillside, spark within my heart
holds onto nothing bigger than a dream
and nothing better for a place to start.

Ignite the hillside! Spark within my heart
melodious strains of valleys steeped in song!
There's nothing better for a place to start
two rights to join, and so correct a wrong.

Melodious strains of valleys steeped in song,
an empty hand in glove, an empty hand
two rights to join, and so correct a wrong
as night falls on the frozen mountain-land.

Shadows

Here is mine and, here, yours;
from our soles, each footfall followed.

Hand in hand, each closing doors'
sound just left me hollowed.

Beneath Wrought Iron Ribs

Beneath wrought iron ribs, Central Station
resounds with arrival, with departure.
The arch of her lip, her wrist, her notation;
these words mark a nascent adventure.

Resounds with arrival, with departure
announcement — Newcastle, Durham, Carlisle.
These words mark a nascent adventure —
Candle, cathedral, centurion — beguile.

Announcement – Newcastle, Durham, Carlisle.
Above ancient stone ribs, bells rhyme —
Candle, cathedral, centurion — beguile.
The clocks and the candles appeal time.

Above ancient stone ribs, bells rhyme,
the air rings with a sense of precession!
The clocks and the candles appeal time
beneath wrought-iron ribs, Central Station.

On Framwellgate Bridge In Late December

The shadow of Cuthbert's finger,
bestows a prayer upon the Wear.
Bathes, with tiger balm, a tincture,
the bruises of the ebbing year.
Two arches; cutwater glasses,
east to Dalton Burn and Seaham,
time and tide forever passes
between Framwellgate in Durham.

Tenor bells sound the afternoon
and haloes cast and common prayers
all bound with holy joy! A new moon,
from blacksmith cloud, appears —
honeyed with spoon song, descanting
and threading stories of this stream
with passages of sky. Enchanting!
And we, passing this mirror, gleam.

Rainbow

Over the drab, dull red-brick houses
a rainbow spans its arc across the sky
heavy with cloud, slate-grey
spectacular, while trees
swayed by winds' envy
brace for rain:

Love
looks like it's happening again...

Between Two Wind-Blown Trees

She sheltered her sheets between two wind-blown trees;
a worn linden and a sapling juniper.
She wrote out her year beneath their dappled leaves,
considering the worth of the words on the paper.

A worn linden and a sapling juniper;
both told their own long-sown tales
and, considering the worth of the words on the paper,
she dreamed her sheets into spinnaker sails.

Both told their own long-sown tales,
from sun-kissed streets to shadowy alleys.
She dreamed her sheets into spinnaker sails
and breathed her poems of hill-tops and valleys,

from sun-kissed streets to shadowy alleys,
she cast off and travelled the beckoning breeze
and, breathing her poems of hill-tops and valleys,
she sheltered her sheets between two wind-blown trees.

Twelfth Night Regards

'Tis spent… this twelfth night, thinking in North Shields,
cigarette smoke shrouds the top shelves, and the tenders,
turning this way and that, regard weekend spenders.
But, beyond, beyond the sound of this uncouth crowd,
at the pissoir, I've spent not a penny,
and I'm laughing out loud!

At the top table, the powerful guilds
with their long faces, regard cups and mutter.
Snugged lovers stare, as jarred candles flare and gutter.
The backs at the bar are bent. But, O…from the cloud,
her presence turns me one-eighty, I bow,
and I'm laughing out loud!

With this archer's glance, the town becomes fields
and shop-fronts, sheeted cotton! Street signs…ancient
trees!
The traffic is wooden; birdsong rills on the breeze.
But, at the river, a fog divine, heavy-browed
descends, takes me prisoner, I miss her.
But I'm laughing out loud!

A Quiver

A quiver of arrows, and I'm all a-shiver
the battlements, the barricades, and barrows gleam
and all the world's a dream
as I hope to deliver

in an arc across the sky
(my aim is true)
in the blinking of an eye
my love, to you.

Archery In The UK

Her arrow rives the wintered bay
and I fall hard on North Parade.
In my Kismet Hardy hat I lay,
wondering her stroke of grace.

And I fall hard on North Parade,
arrow riveting my ear, my air;
wondering her stroke of grace.
And of it? Oh, I'd grin, I swear!

Arrow riveting my ear, my air;
sober on the old red sofa.
And of it? Oh, I'd grin, I swear.
Scent of Cumbrian juniper.

Sober on the old red sofa,
listening to Drinking In L.A.
Scent of Cumbrian Juniper.
Her arrow rives the wintered bay.

A Thimble Of Poetry

"He went to sea in a thimble of poetry." – Poet Warning, Jim Harrison

He cast off early
just as dawn was breaking
saw the blues there, saw the greens
dreamed the clouds were Kingdoms ruled
by distant Kings and Queens.

He'd often wondered
what it took to get there
this airy realm, this realm of mist and ice
to feel the cloudburst on his skin
like breath of paradise.

He cast his net wide
took in sea-brack, blown-in
flotsam, things that people leave
out on the beach to travel with
the tide's incessant weave.

He wove their stories
like a winter cloak, hardwearing
weathered with fabled centuries.
From pieces of their lives he made
enduring histories.

He wrote mine down too
wrote it down and sung it
wistful, dreaming on the breeze
that somehow it might reach my heart
beyond those swelling seas.

Where The Yew Trees Grow

The longbow, the instruction in and of,
was once integral to (I've read in books)
a young man's education.
Knights, old by half my age,
with knotted fingers, eyes faded,
would lead the jacks to the quiet wood,
the wild boar acre, where the yew trees grow,
where Centurions and Vikings before drew blood,
marking selected barks with chalked x's.

Hescho Peech

hescho peech
becomes you
wear it like a spell
threaded beach-find
binds you
cones of pineal
hescho peech
burns bergamot
walks a country mile
bewilderment of bon mots
in the northern isles
hescho peech
unordinary
seldom is she seen
a shadow rose
on summer lawns
washing over me
hescho peech
a rhythm
an echo in the hall
letters learnt by repetition
written on the wall
hescho peech
reminds me
to ink, to love,
to speak, to daub
between the sheets

and through these journals
hescho peech
pens postcards
treasure found
unexpected
in the inbox
tapping at the x

Her Pianist Toes

Not in any schooled way do I play, but
from her pianist toes I finger loose
a free-form primitive jazz; mingus-hot,
denuding crude runs of cool delta blues.

Reflections In Chrome

Settled in water, we shape, and beneath
candlelit sheet of perfume, we steam
hips, ribs, spine and shins with no space between.
I write you as reflections in chrome.

Of the Ouse, the Tyne, the Wear, we weave
slow-flowing poems of their cool streams –
We threshold their bridges, seek margins unseen:
I write them as reflections in chrome.

The same air as saints and blue bloods we breathe
in cathedrals and cafés, on bridges, in dream.
The same shape, we bathe, you and me; we lean.
I write us as reflections in chrome.

Prismatic

I.
Tin soldiers march
across a field of felt
regimental red, not bleeding.

II.
Blue light blooms
a cross upon the crypt wall
grooved columns like some ancient dial.

III.
Iron wheels of heavy industry
draw your eye
between the spokes, a flash of orange.

IV.
I love wallpaper patterned with dancing birds
You say *'s'gone* thank goodness
not *'s'goan*.

V.
I walk with my head in the clouds
yet it is you, with eyes close to the ground
who shows me heaven.

Stippling

I.
Haiku littering the high street
paper lanterns blushing fruit trees
favourite corduroy cowboy shirt.

II.
Five pale horses encircle her
flat stones stipple millpond surface
tomorrow bows her narrow back.

III.
Many years had passed since then
his echoes gathered like ghost crowds:
Such language! She giggled and she sighed.

IV.
The blood black around his grin
penny-eyed glued to the paving
her calf her brow half shadowed.

V.
The wet magic of the well rope
the old world is now just memory
still the Spanish mountains sparkle.

Exceptional

I.
Lemonade tang
fizz on my tongue
dancing bubbles.

II.
Rain rattles glass
or was it the wind's
cold whispering?

III.
A heart carved into
a wooden chair
denotes a Swiss hotel room.

IV.
The sky's on fire
2000 m up
above Granada.

V.
Four out of five senses fail me
I breathe in the darkness
rich fragrances of you.

I Hear Beethoven

When you touch me
I hear Beethoven:
your fingers
playing up and down my spine
with deftness of a virtuoso
you caress
cadenzas out of me
our bodies harmonised
in runs of contrapuntal melody
riotous concerto
no sweeter sound than this
music to me.

A Poem Called

Tapping at the keyboard tiles
— in the glow of the evening,
pausing only for some hours;
once to find inspiration
in an unexpected shower
and once again, to take a bath —
these selected letters became
these collected words; becoming
a poem called *steaming bao buns*.

Her Frequency

Piano play with her toes
finger poems from her flow
slim limbs shimmer bubbled foam
I'd grin every morning.

To her bedside I would bring
several lovesongs I should sing
brown paper packages tied up with string
messages under her pillow.

Magic numbers sweet surprise
unencumbered by her sighs
across the counties I would fly
one hundred thousand arrows.

Above the birdsong buzzing bees
betwixt between two wind-blown trees
beneath the sheeted melodies
her frequency her glow her dreams.

Drawn

Tiptoed the tight lines of this night
with gifted eye and double-you:
All the dark gowns fell away.
'Wear your bluest socks, my lover;
wear your Spanish cotton crown.'
We bent toward the dawn in flower,
and, together, we were drawn.

Penning

The birds have yet to wake or start singing
but from the dawn she draws this morning
a yard of muse — sans roman rhyming —
in her kitchen, while there is warming
loose leaf Ginseng, a croissant; bringing
to her ribs the special drawer, enquiring
of a postcard within, begins penning:
He summoned to Rydal Mount one morning,
the maid, the monkeys and the muse…

Dawn Resonance

Beneath my window, soft birdsong
plays in my garden, all along
the treeline: sweet, melodic, low
'For I have lovéd you so long'
the lyric chimes with sounds below:
soft birdsong beneath my window

as I awake from this sweet dream
warmed from within, though no sunbeam
appears, its dawning breath to take
without a dazzle or a gleam
I drink you in, my thirst to slake
from this sweet dream, as I awake

I am so fortunate to find
space to pen love songs in my mind
while outside, day is growing late:
the school bell beckons on the wind
and duty calls me to the gate
to find I am so fortunate.

I Coo

On this pearl-hued afternoon
wrapped in our tumbled bed, I coo
a sandman courting borrowed time
this beret lends me some Sassoon —
I coo your toes in blue wool or shoe
or not too much; I stand to rhyme
fall into the evening'd sofa.
We've been writing for an hour
I coo our cathedral chime.

St Mary's I

Cathedral bells pealing out, tolling the hour
as love not unholy spills down like a shower
of rain on the hillside baked year upon year
to be slaked by the flow as you lie with me here

and birdsong, sweet birdsong at our window wide
descanting, plain-chanting the bell-song's cascade
I love you, I love you resounds through the air
where we meet, disembodied, yet find ourselves there:

Cathedral of water, Cathedral of fire
Cathedral of earth? Or Cathedral of air?
Cathedral of death in the arms of my lover
who lingers long after, aglow with me here.

St Mary's II

Vertiginous winding to the lighthouse top
where the weak or faint-hearted are tempted to stop
pressing on, ever on, up the ladder we climb
to look over the seascape remembered in rhyme

and I do, and I do want to stand with you here
looking over the Bay every year after year
as the seagulls below us who bask in the sun
have their fish still to catch, we have work to be done

weaving poetry, spiralling throughout our lives
telling tales of the townspeople, husbands and wives
and their children who play in the rockpools below
singing songs of the past, to the future we grow.

Two Poets In The Park

Two poets in the park
eating mango sorbet
sipping coffee
holding hands and dreaming poets' dreams.

Two poets in the park
sitting down beside the fountain
watching the world trickle by
so beautiful it seems.

Two poets in the park
honeymooning
lovesong-crooning
people passing by, just let them stare.

Two poets in the park
weave word-webs
in and out the dusty bluebells
down between the daffodils they are

two poets in the park
lain side by side and whispering
their ballads, secret sonneteering, music of
two poets after dark.

Vessels Sheeted

Above the mountain lakes she strides
in sleep beneath the moon in honour
of the morning song of sparrows
cloistered choir of the hedgerow
or the little monkeys' chatter
to the coming Easter Sunday.
Waves unfolding one another
like the pages of his novel
fallen at the bedside table
vessels sheeted sleeping lover
at the window finger rhythms
on the glass a spilled sea of dreams

&

so fast the constellations slide
across the northern city sky
with Venus rising one inch under
cover — my Queen of Cumbria —
climbs beyond the dotted river
to the hem and crosses over
in her orange brocade and boots.

Easter Sonnet Revisited

You wrote me a sonnet at Easter time
sent it across the sea in binary
from heart, to mind, to hand, to heart-of-mine
perhaps, you thought, inconsequentially

but words possess a power all their own
born in the heart, and whispered on the lips
which, reaching the receiver works upon
with subtle charm, her writer's fingertips

and so, she places tips to keys and pens
a perfect answer, in response to this
and letting down her guard, one day she sends
that answer, sealed within a keystroked kiss:

From word-play such as this, new love is born
at Easter, time of reincarnation…

Regarding An Easter Sonnet

A year has passed since he was last
beneath her Roman garden borne:
twelve moons in shadow have been cast
and gently, stirred leaves on the lawn.

Reborn, he found himself no more
alone among the crowd, but perched
at the toes of her piano:
The prelude to their coupled verse.

In Edinburgh — her name revealed —
Rolled the stone, strolled royal miles.
Then, still, before Ross fountain, spilled
words and wishes; kisses; smiles.

Durham — sweet Durham's river clear —
where dreams are dreamt and soaps gifted,
carillon bells peal out the year,
and the lovers' hearts are lifted.

The morning sun on York Minster,
is risen; I grind; robust; sanguine.
I turn and bite my thumb* at Caesar.
"Your voice falls hollow to my Queen."

[*a nod toward The Bard is made: *R&J*; A1 S1]

Dreamer's Delights

Your eyes, the colour of the North Sea on a stormy day
your teasing smile, and all the sunshine in it.

Your dreamer's profile, tracing outlines of the boy
whose Artist's hands trace pleasures without limit.

Your shape, aligned with mine, in sacred sleeping
time out of mind, the rhythm of our dreaming.

Tonight, Together, Apart

At four forty-four this a.m. I broke
from a curious and troublesome dream:
a back yard cold hound arced from a choke,
bejewelling black glass with sad bark and stream.

Struggle, the chain enchanted. But relief?
Not tonight. Nor evasion. Fear defeat.
The fettered dog's howl and shackle of teeth
seemed to goad no one but me in the street.

I spoke. I scolded the chain and dark cur.
Silence, night stealers! Deliver release!
I crave the heat and heart of my lover.
I ache to favour, to follow, to please.

I woke at last — the window, reflected
the shape of my love; a vision, complete.
She slept at home and roamed a laked district,
sparkled naked beneath Rydal Mount's sheet.

Night searcher: I seek her, combing the deep.
I see her. I'll reach her Cumbrian gleam
tomorrow! Tomorrow? This dog will sleep.
Tonight, together, apart, he shall dream.

Two Collared Doves

I saw two collared doves at Hesket Newmarket
cloud-coloured collared doves crossing the road
one leaned its feathered head towards the other
to share some secret wish, lighten a load:

I loved you then, she cooed (coo-cooed)
I love you still, cooed he
in such a manner, they were wooed,
would ever-lovéd be.

It was a market day in early summer,
a sultry, pollen-heavy market day
when one dove pledged her love unto the other
who joined his heart to hers most willingly.

The people on the green drank ale and hollered
the doves crossing the road paid them no heed
for deep in love they were, feathered and collared
of human praise or censure, had no need.

They nested in the eves or in the rafters
it little mattered, now that they were paired
they cooed of clouds, and dreams and ever-afters
since they crossed that bright day, such dreams they shared.

Jubilee Floats

Jubilee floats trundle over the rumbling road
on past the village green
bunting flaps the telegraph poles,
slaps time to the rhythm of the children's clapping
swallows dive and plough the sky,
while candyfloss clouds build and tumble:
I miss you, only miles away,
but feel your love surround me like a blanket,
weighted with magic,
sparkling with cloth of gold.

From Nicholas To Jubilee

After making love, we drove
around the greatest city in the world
(for access to the Lakes). You pointed
out the citadel and cathedral, painted
childhood haunts as gold, wove passages
that, on your lips, appointed
saints with majesty.

Re/Birthday

Then, all at once, and everywhere,
an explosion, a mighty crash,
tore the restaurant asunder,

momentarily waking me,
or willing me to sip further
the elixir she held to me,

and the birthday began again.
Rice, like wedding confetti, fell
from above and I was reborn.

Birdsong

Every day, I waken to birdsong.
Sometimes the lark and thrush, sweet twittering
or the sparrow and the chaffinch, cheerful chattering
or the rook, cawing in raucous symphony:
signature calls, all poetry to me.

Your touch draws out a different kind of birdsong
low moaning, from a hollow deep in me
transformed through love into a holy plainsong
where never sin, nor pain, nor wrong could be:

just simple beauty, couched in bowered bliss
the thrillsong of a passion whispered soft,
rough-smoothly sung through barely parted lips
not any more, nor any less, than this.

This Song Of Sparrows

Unopened, dun letters envelop the floor.
Sheaf leaflets, none read; too many to mention…
But her hand, delivered today to my door —
penned, posted, scented — receives full attention.

 Her lines bring pleasure to me, and I tease
nuance from her *Wish You Were Here* missives.
News from the mill, the hill; river, and trees.
'I will, and shall, return. I send kisses.'

I miss her, I whisper. So I conjure
and raise Cuthbert's Causeway, macadam
our passage, our birdsong adventure;
sweet breeze of honey; unimagined.

June thirteenth, her paved shadow, first rising,
aslant in glass, brushes chrome in umbra;
blushes my morning through noon, producing
a cool breeze, implausible last summer.

I light a jarred candle and write her:
Tonight the room shallows, throws shadows, and grows…
I invite her. Come, lay by my fire.
Kiss, address, send her, *this song of sparrows.*

Glittering

The Bay has taken on the shape of summer;
high-cloud clears to sparkle-tip the waves:
glittering prize bequeathed to us in winter
when ice-cold breaths warmed into brighter days.

I'm falling ever deeper like the surf-swell
plummets towards the depths of this salt sea
sand underfoot I stand, glowing and grateful:
golden, the love your heart has gifted me.

My mind's expansive, spinning like a dancer
pirouetting, setting sorrows free
past pains inscribed upon a dusty ledger
erased by love's all-healing potency:

You are my east, my sunrise and my rest
I take with you, couched in my bowered west.

Atlantic Beadlet Anemone

I found jewels in a barnacled crevice
within the cracked rocks on Cullercoats beach
teetering close to the pools like a novice
saltwater gems within reach.

I found gold in the liminal lightspace
in the little-boy-blue of your eyes
in the smile on my son's cherubic face
in the sea with its pull, with its sighs.

I found peace in the sea-plain littoral
peace and joy, which arose as it fell
in the shore-meadows, dazzlingly floral
in the cove carved out by the tide-swell.

In the arc of this day I found heaven
anchored here by the pull of the earth
I give thanks for such gifts freely given
in this summer of love's bright rebirth.

How The Arrow Flew

Beauty drew the archer's eye; absolutely true.
"To this woman," bade the bowman. How the arrow flew!
As a vesper, as a whisper; diaphanous, and blue
as Venus rising in the window; under waxing moon.

White Heaven

Underneath the skies of this white heaven
marionettes dance
dip and bow
crawl
mount a lamppost
scare the children.

Seagulls on sticks stalk
jellyfish catchers
catch them unawares
the children's faces
glittering, are painted.

At the bar, a hen-night princess
appears as a mirage
or haze of nylon taffeta
and disappears into a fruited cider
where would-be princesses admire her
captures her knight-errant, entombs him in a castle tower.

Underneath the skies of this white heaven
I see your eyes
in the colour and cast of this blue-agate sea
send messages in bottles, binary
upon the tide-swell daydreams dazzle
digitally
daring
to
fly
free.

Beach Of Dubious Pleasures

I.
Peeling-paint
Art-deco buildings
faded glory.

II.
Fluorescent daubs
fibreglass moulding
60s Alice.

III.
Queues form
a holding area
at the fall of Rome.

IV.
Wood cracks
tracks held on by rusted nails
rollercoasting.

V.
Your eyes sparkle
making the whole day
worth the entrance fee.

Beneath The Big Dipper

I.
The Pepsi sippers smear
beneath the big dipper
Blackpool between my ears.

II.
Pleasure beach, love is here
beneath the big dipper.
I heart oompah-pah bears.

III.
Carousel riders rear
beneath the big dipper
pennants of palms and hair.

IV.
Lichtenstein clings to her
beneath the big dipper
she wows this day tripper.

V.
The sea, the sky, the pier.
Beyond the big dipper
I write, wish you were here.

The Summer Of Love And Fresh Air

It was the summer of love and fresh air.
God knows how we made it through,
with barely two red cents to rub together:
you lit up my smile, did up my hair.

We took trips with the children
packed sandwiches
didn't worry about the rain
ran free through parks and gardens,
the next morning, did it all over again.

Collapsed, exhausted, heaped beneath the sheets
woke early, sought out one another's lips:
as I breathed in the scent of you,
you held my hands, my hips...

We managed it! Not only did we manage, we
excelled — 'cost of living crisis' and 'austerity'
cage-words to tame the fire in you and me
while all the while, defiantly we
burned brighter.

Fairytale Of Northumberland

Camelot towers tall above
the river where we walk
our senses are attuned to love;
our tongues, to lovers' talk.

Afternoon sun, meandering
through a haze of August heat
beats time to lovers' wandering
and measures of delight.

Such days as in a dream I pass
with you, happily spent
as salmon leap, the air to bless
in frenzied merriment.

Just as my heart leaps at your kiss,
caresses upon waking
your silhouette, profiled in this
moment: ours for the taking.

I Whispered

I once found a fluted glass at the foot
of a door in a beautiful city
where morning sunlight spilled through the Lindens
like ghosts lining the streets and I whispered
a name that was still unknown to me then
but one day poured from your lips to my ears
turned in slow motion a ring song sang out
on an anvil and the air vibrated.

Top Dollar

I will dress in fresh clean
white tee shirt and scruffy jeans.
Scuffed-up monkey boots
don't mean I can't pop my collar.

Unbox socks of cotton.
No, I ain't forgotten how
to tie my laces, I was shown.
Yeah, my hair needs cutting.

Wash my face this morning.
Pay the rent tomorrow.
Splash my favourite cologne
as if it cost top dollar.

Ride the train to Central.
Greet you at our coffee shop.
Carry your bags for you.
The bed is made, the cupboard stocked.

The rooms are clean and scented.
You don't care much for such things.
But I will play guitar and sing
for you a song presented…

From Cairo To Carlisle

The night before our wedding vows
were exchanged, we changed the bedding.
Cotton from Cairo to Carlisle, you said.
And, amid these mills and pyramids
unfolded, tucked and spread, we slept.

Dreamed freedoms formed from enslavements;
cold words are never sentenced here.
We have no need for apple crops,
tobacco shops, or any other
pavements. Watch dusking sparrows stave
for us, elder tree arrangements.

Our slew of gifts; featherlight
glyphs, handwritten and secreted
between sheets, writhen; scented letters.
The rings beside us on the table;
bedside for this evening only.
Raiment waiting on the railing.
The morning birdsong, wedding bells.

This Stunning Creature

A salmon, glistening, unexpected,
in silver breastplate armour, unprotected,
rose from the unseen other realm, breathed

once upon this August mirror, ecstatic
at the vision found there, arched, brief
in sunlight — beneath the river, disappeared

just as the bells of St. Lawrence
pealed the final quarter tones of the hour,
concentric circles on air and water.

We spoke in exclamation of this stunning creature,
both fleeting and forever; the Coquet
rent and sealed again, two realms with, dare I speak it?

Yes.
I do.
A kiss.

I sign and dot this with ellipses…
One evening, late September.

This Crossing Of Realms

From crystal screen to crystal screen
across the shining sea
one kingdom to another
where you wooed and wedded me:

from west to east, expansive
riding rails and playing tunes,
a pot of tea then pizza to
multiple honeymoons.

From mirror into mirror,
a thousand stories shared,
an otherworldly visitor
who blessed, then disappeared

into the sacred river Coquet
like the Tyne, or Wear
above the former, where we met
the latter, we drew near.

From one kiss to ten thousand
crossing realm to peerless realm
lips upon lips to seal with this
your blessing, bond and balm.

Honeymoon Night

Star-spangled bathing
in honey-lit moonglow:
I do so love you so
I do so love you so.

The sheets how they ripple
and rise as our sighs grow
replete, I love you so
repeat, I love you so.

Our bodies entangled
our minds even more so
complete, I love you oh
so sweet, I love you so.

The candlelight flickers and flares
trickles tallow
temptation's so sweet—oh
I do so love you so.

As husband and wife
we awake on the morrow
'I do' and 'I will' so
I'll always love you so.

Our honeymoon song's
taken up by the sparrow:
I do so love you so
I do so love you so.

Vermeer

Beyond a blue-red, orange-grey
sock peeking from beneath the duvet,
the room appeared, to me, arranged
by Vermeer, perhaps, or some old master.

The silent curtain partly drawn.

Within a still life lance of day-
light, her slip, errant, her ribs, displayed,
neat, plated, late season berries,
the morning before Michaelmas; a young maid.

Duet

I sing my heart out to you:
not muted nor flamboyant.
Still, where your words or kisses stop it
steady, as the pattern of our love.

Measured in calm, considered tones
not coarse nor laboured
calling across coloured coasts
ascending mountains, carrying us home.

You play a lover's rock and roll
not rigid nor restrained,
just strumming rhythms heard in dreams
foot-tapping time to heartbeats in a bar.

We sing a duet
soft and strident: *a-cappella* love
rising through eaves
ascends the arc of autumn skies above.

Labouring

Burning early morning wax,
brings forth a daughter of the Muse:

See now she comes
and how she sings
a thousand I-Love-Yous...

When The Named Storms Come

When the named storms come
and the power lines are down
and our channels of communication have been cut
how will you contact me?

I will be reaching out to you, and you
will mirror me, who reaches out
even now, even as I write this
in the dark.

When the named storms come
again, you'll send a letter:
I am sure you will
and hope the postal service doesn't falter

and I will write a poem
like lovers did in bygone times
and seal it in a lipsticked envelope
addressed in my inked hand

and if the post can't make it through
then I will drive to you
and if I can't get petrol
I will ride my bike

from coast to coloured coast
and you will greet me on the bridge
at mouth of Tyne, our lips will meet
after the storm is done:

I will still love you when the named storms come.

Spellcasting

Bewitched pigs
flaming leaves
bent, twisted twigs,
a wind which weaves,
mourns, moans of melody
haunts with its poetry
hand-in-hand you-and-me
walking a gold-coin trimmed alley
through the cold veil of autumn.

All this heat and symmetry
remembered, how the
breath peals, wreathed in mist
encircling this
sacred geometry.

Today is heavy:
rain falls and you aren't here
I call up the crystal screen
stare hard into and
through the ubiquitous ether,
hover a finger
conjure you hither.

I Long To Belong

I long to be long
in your arms
in your hand-hold
my love
how I long to belong.

I long to be bold
with your charms
measured tenfold
my love
how I long to be bold.

I love to be loved
by your caresses blessed
how I love to be loved
my beloved.

So I'm ending my song
with a kiss and a blessing
I wait
where I long to belong.

Incandescence

The shadows rise, the sunlight falls
and all's aglow, within these walls:
the candlelight, the cold, the heat.
the candlelight, the cold, the heat.

Sheets ripple, springs ache for release
I am for you, who aims to please
resistance fails, our rising falls
rebounds the room, resound — the halls

alight, alight! We come alive
beneath the sheets, beyond we dive
into a higher, sacred state
of candlelight, and cold, and heat.

Her Hymn In Waltz Time

I will remember. A rhyme yet to come.
All is rhythm. Horn and drum.
It was autumn. I will remember.

A rhyme yet to come. Glance her mirror.
All is beauty. Glimpse and glimmer.
It was November. A rhyme yet to come.

All is rhythm. Six bells chime.
All is hum. Her hymn in waltz time.
It was evensong. All is rhythm.

Horn and drum. The town crier.
All is harmonic. Field and fire.
It was the Beaver moon. Horn and drum.

It was autumn. The spaces between.
All is calm. Tea lights and leaves.
It was a low sun. It was autumn.

I will remember. A rhyme yet to come.
All is rhythm. Horn and drum.
It was autumn. I will remember.

Returning To The Northlands

Returning to The Northlands on a plane
through cloud
the engines shake and shudder
wings judder
my heart in my throat as
we touch down.

Returning to The Northlands once again
this time, I will not go back
not if it takes my every bone's
refusal and
though I may go insane.

My realm, and my terrain:
within the wings, a King-in-Waiting
reaches out,
extends an Artist's hand,
declares, 'You're real!'

Your realm is mine, now rise
and seal this bond
as we stand firm, together
learning one another
yearning, ever, Love
returning to The Northlands.

Reborn Again

All across the land echoes a brand new morn[1]
I am reborn in you, I am reborn
A frosted hand in glove, though weather-worn
thaws, graven with signs of how I've grown.

I am reborn in you, I am reborn
the lake lies golden under winter's crown
then thaws, graven with signs of how I've grown
a mirrored ice-rink glass I dance upon.

The lake lies golden under winter's crown
a honeyed moon blesses the horizon
a mirrored ice-rink glass I dance upon
hand in hand in love, never alone.

A honeyed moon blesses the horizon
a frosted hand in glove, though weather-worn
walks hand in hand in love, never alone:
all across the land echoes a brand new morn.

---

1   Inspired by the song 'When A Child Is Born' by Fred Jay

Sonnet (Bus To Dungeon Ghyll)

Sonnet, woven over poets' weekend,
to birdsong, kisses, blue socks, caresses;
long baths, silk scarves and Lichtenstein dresses.
Vacate the room by eleven a.m.

On honeymoon sheets. The duvet is penned
by second breakfast: Zimmerman verses;
the cadence of their kitchen voices.
Bend the bow, release; villanelle ascend

the roads and bridges of Northumbria.
Greetings from Alnmouth. Greetings, I will
send letters, almost rhyming couplets,
odes to Durham, Hexham, Edinburgh.

Five rivers, and the bus to Dungeon Ghyll.
Woven over poets' weekend: Sonnet.

The Wintered Queen

Into the crystal screen, the Wintered Queen
with heart encased in ice, gazes:
begins to dance throughout the changing scene
while rain, rooftops and pavements glazes

glides over a bridge above the Tyne
with a familiar stranger
mirror upon mirror intertwined
King into Queen, St Nicholas to Grainger.

A mirage or a vision, carousel
appears before them — hovers
with fairytale cast, and, as by some spell
enchanted, they fall, soon to become lovers:

Their hearts, their art, two arcs across the sky
inscribed within this book of poetry.

Publication Credits

The cadralore "Prismatic", "Stippling" and "Exceptional" were first published in Gleam Magazine's *Journal of the Cadralor* (Issue IV, June 2022)

"The Summer Of Love And Fresh Air" was first published online at Spillwords Press (August 2022)

"Duet" was first published online at MasticadoresUSA (September 2022)

"When The Named Storms Come" was first published online at MasticadoresUSA (September 2022)

"Fairytale Of Northumberland" was first published in *Free Verse Revolution: A Literary Magazine* (Issue VII, September 2022)

The poems "Re/Birthday" and "Atlantic Beadlet Anemone" appear in *Free Verse Revolution: A Literary Magazine* (Issue VIII, December 2022)

Also Available From EIF
(via Amazon and in selected bookstores)

40 Poems At 40 by Ingrid Wilson
ISBN: 9781739757700

40 Poems is the debut poetry collection from Ingrid Wilson. It is poetry of place and space, and here lie the clues and the beauty to Wilson's poetry. Her work is charted, landscaped, travelled, explorative and laden with adventure. There are bright, sad, dreamy postcards telling of the beauty of Barcelona, the slate-grey, but singing, county of Cumbria, Malaga, 'the emptiness' of Manchester, 'the fields' of London, 'the ancient pasts' of Newcastle, the mysterious beauty of Slovenia, Venice and its lullaby… lapping water is never far from her ear.

A reflective, rich debut that reveals, in startling images and with dextrous word-play, a trove for those of us learning to live and to love.

Wounds I Healed: The Poetry of Strong Women
edited by Gabriela Marie Milton
ISBN: 9781739757724

Award-winning authors, Pushcart nominees, emerging poets, voices of women and men, come to the fore in this stunning, powerful, and unique anthology. These poems testify both to the challenges that women face in our society, and to their power to overcome them. A memorable collection of over 200 poems by more than 100 authors, this anthology is a must-have for all lovers of poetry. We all can benefit from the poetry of survival, and of healing. We all can benefit from the experiences so beautifully evoked in this book. We can all come together to emerge triumphant from pain.

Nature Speaks of Love and Sorrow by Jeff Flesch
ISBN: 9781739757755

In this hotly-anticipated debut poetry collection from Jeff Flesch, the author invites us to take a voyage with him through trauma and pain into acceptance and bliss in the embrace of nature itself. Jeff's poems are infused with the textures and colours of the natural world, and his journey through this sensory paradise provides the backdrop to his inner journey towards healing and growth.

Three-Penny Memories, A Poetic Memoir
by Barbara Harris Leonhard
ISBN: 9781739757762

"Do you love your mother?"
— This provocative question provides the catalyst for this stunning poetic memoir from Barbara Harris Leonhard. Through her artfully-crafted poetry, the author considers where her love and loyalties lie following her aging mother's diagnosis with Alzheimer's.

Printed in Great Britain
by Amazon

18783600R00058